# A

# GLORIOUS

# POETIC

# RAGE

# A

# GLORIOUS

# POETIC

# RAGE

~ POEMS ~

elmo shade

*atmosphere press*

For all First Responders
who sacrificed their lives, families, and personal health
in the battle against COVID-19

and

For all who peacefully protested
during the Black Lives Matter movement
and continue to fight against racism and racial inequality

# TABLE OF CONTENTS

# POETRY IS

the romance of time.

the displacement of silence in a world full of noise.

an audience of strangers.

knowing that the pain now is part of the happiness then.

an understanding that there is no such thing as what might have been.

a form of expression for those who are unable to say one thing at a time.

staring all day at a blank sheet without writing a single line.

a musical instrument that plays notes in perfect concert with the beating of the heart.

a connection with the human, the non-human, the physical and the metaphysical.

gazing out the kitchen window into the beauty or the terror.

every color autumn tree leaves display and each

gentle descent to a frozen ground.

a way of forgiveness that can look at any situation with total gratitude.

healing from loss and the resilience to rise up and out of the muddy water.

connecting with others

so they can keep their mop

in the closet more often.

# FIRST LESSON IN POETRY

I am old enough to remember
Mary Chapin Carpenter singing,
"I'm the Opening Act".

Actually, some opening acts
should have been headliners.
And some headliners
should have stayed sober.

The first lesson in poetry
is don't give up your day job.
The second lesson is
don't take rejection personally.

Rejection is a lot like being
the opening act. Poems get
written and read only without
the standing ovation at the end.

Often, the standing ovation
is watching some opening acts
become headliners and some
headliners become laureates.

Like Tracy K. Smith, Billy Collins,
W.S. Merwin and the Stones--
I seriously doubt Mick and Keith
were ever the opening act.

For now, I'll patiently wait in line
as your opening act and seriously
promise to stay sober.

# TWO WIDOWS HAVING COFFEE

Soft gray hair
Worn silver bands
Seated at a two-top
Neither looking at their phones.

I can't hear them and
I don't read lips so
guessing their chat is
of grandkids and pets.

One gently sips her coffee
while the other talks continuously,
then stops as they both
stare out the front window.

Dressed to the nines
Pierced earrings and boots.
Each with gray down vests
keeping their conversation warm.

I slowly rise and walk by
to attend to nature's business,
overhearing one softly say,
"I felt like killing the fucker!"

# LOW BATTERY

These devices. What good are they
if not smart enough
to stay alive?  A constant drain,
green bar turning yellow,

yellow shrinking to red,
and if you're not paying attention,
going into cardiac arrest.

Remembering to pack these
life support lines when you can't
remember to pack your toothbrush
is a constant dilemma.

Why not go back
to the Pony Express days,
the Wild West version of the 10X,
the lone rider, leathered saddle bags
full of emails and dot coms.

You'll see him coming from a distance
in a dust bowl, his horse's hooves
in cadence with your impatience.

And when he arrives, you'll reach
for your string-tied treasures
as he pulls them back
asking first for your password.

# PROCESSIONARY CATERPILLARS

imagine
a merry-go-round of
caterpillars circling
a flower pot rim
like westward wagons
unaware of food
close by
in the center, blindly
following leader's
long suicide procession,
round and round-
caterpillars
slowly starving,
inching towards
the sea searching
for salt safe to drink

# TWO VOICES OF A PANDEMIC

I see humans scurrying about consumed in fear
*(I feel the emotion of fear knowing that I am NOT my fear)*

I listen to the media and political pundits competing for ratings
*(I listen for what I know is TRUE and mute the rest)*

I see playgrounds empty of children and restaurants CLOSED
*(I enjoy family game time and learn new recipes together)*

I smell imminent death in every direction
*(I smell the freshness of Spring and the crispness of bacon)*

I miss my favorite sport teams and playoffs
*(I read 100 pages and walk 10,000 steps every day)*

I go stir-crazy with the endless social isolation
*(I'm connected to my on-line community)*

I spread xenophobic hate on social media with my demands
*(I spread love, joy, wonder, and wisdom to all beings)*

# SUNSHINE QUARANTINE

Today, the warmth of the sun
plays a symphony to the sky.

Balcony conversations crescendo
with music and the laughter

of children drawing rainbows
full of yellow, purple, and reds.

And, after days of labor
lifting the spirits of the lambs,

the sun takes its rest. And I,

stepping out into the rain,
know that I am never the rain.

I am the sun. I am the laughter.
I am the symphony that plays
long after the darkness comes.

The rain once felt cold and gray,
but today, it feels wonderful.

# PREDATOR

The Predator is invisible
to the naked eye. It only
reveals itself
days after it strikes.

It travels as a high-jacker,
not on highways but
through the air.

It sees you even if
you are covered in debris
or in disregard.

It shows no mercy
as it steals your breath,
your smell, your taste, or
your will to survive.

But its fate is pre-determined,
its weakness your strength,
its enemy your ally.

It cannot survive the crushing weight
of never giving up.

# IF YOU WERE REALLY HERE
*For Elisha*


I awaken and the air of your absence
from the next room
leaves me gasping for breath.

A made bed, a closet full of voices
I never heard or understood.

What would I say to you now
if you were really here?

I'm sorry. I wish I had known
the depth of your darkness.

Is it any wonder that I failed to hear
your tender soul crying for help?

Is there any way I can tell you how much
you are missed, how much you are loved,

how much sweetness your life lives
in each breath we take?

I search the depth of my heart and
still, I cannot find the words...

only these...

forgive me.

That's what I would say
if you were really here.

# R.S.V.P.

A young girl
once told me
she could hopscotch
faster than the
demons chasing her.
So I bought
some colored chalk,
drew squares on
a sidewalk court
in pinks, blues,
and greens, then
sent invitations out
to the make-believe
children who had
no place to play.

# DAY 67 OF A PANDEMIC

City streets mostly empty, sidewalks
have become freeways, houses
sanctuaries, hospitals mortuaries.

Phone apps fill virtual rooms with familiar faces.

The homeless dance in Esther's Park with
little regard for distance as Joe Walsh sings
"Life's been good to me so far".

Cracks in the park's pavement look like
varicose veins while oak acorns and
tiny branches ford their reckless run.

Isolation deepens. Like witnessing a death,
there is no getting back to normal.

Not now. Maybe never.

Today's agenda:

A morning walk alone
An afternoon drive-thru coffee
Day 67...so far.

# WAIT FOR IT

The black crow caws twice
then waits

Then again once
and waits

Then back to twice, then once,
then twice again
and waits

Poets wait for words
tulips for spring

Questions wait for answers
that wait for the grade

Children wait for permission
the infected for a cure

I want my life back, you say
there is no cure
but to wait for it

The black crow caws twice,
then again once

Flying off unanswered,
never to return

# LOVE DOGS (an Ode to Rumi)

No longer a ghost town, only
tumbleweed connections of
suffocating strangers. An Airedale
just ate out of my hand after shaking it.
Pollen floats through the air like ashes
raised from the grave. Yellow-tinted
windshields pass slowly, unsure
of any destination.
Unfamiliar sounds in all directions-
Pendulums swinging
Metronomes ticking
Cash registers ringing
Shops slowly awaken from
a pandemic sleep's sweat. Voices
fill once silent streets with laughter.
Life as we knew it did not forsake us.
Rather, like a dog moaning for its master,
it was us yearning for each other.

# BREAKING NEWS

There is no perfect poem.
There are no innocent angels.
The devil exists only in your heart.
You have to choose your side---
you are either on the Helping team
or the Hurting team.
Sin is a 4-letter word that
insults my intelligence.
I do know the difference between
a beggar and a bigot.
Be kind to whoever waits your table.
Get the flu shot.
Make your bed. It's the state of your head.
Skip a meal...maybe two.
Laugh every day, mostly at yourself.
Drink more coffee.
Wash your hands.
Wear a t-shirt that says something
about what or who you love.
Learn one new word each week
and use it in a spoken sentence.
Remember your Barista's name
Boredom is simply depression
with good P.R.
Play some Bon Iver.
Spend more time with a tree
than with a T.V.
Not flossing is like taking a shower
without washing your armpits.
You don't have to own a pet
to be kind to them.
Sit there. Don't just do something.
Know that it is perfectly fine
some days to just say, "F*ck it!

# I CAN'T QUITE PUT MY FINGER ON IT

but something is amiss
not quite right,

as if there were such a thing-
right or not quite right.

the world wears crooked
like a twice-broken nose,

civility withered & crushed
from a face-first fall.

so heavy for limp legs,
we struggle to stand.

is harvesting hate
this winter's wheat?

is it the earth screaming,
"i can't breathe"

or some other voice?

a clay pot drops from a roof
but does not break.

the anchorman says,
*"and now in other news".*

a young son rushes in to hug the
legs of his war-absent father.

# IS THIS THE WORLD I WANT TO SEE?

Is this the world I want to see?
My mind an attack dog
Salivating for justice.
I see only the perishable.
I see nothing that will last.

Is this the world I want to see?
What I see cannot be real.
What I see can. not. be. real.
His neck has been broken.
Her palms are bleeding out.

Is this the world I want to see?
There is no order of difficulty in peace.
No form of fear that can heal our wounds.
Nothing real can ever be threatened.
Nothing unreal exists.

Is this the world I want to see?
Tin soldiers and buildings burning.
Standing down on our knees.
Down on graveled graves.
*I can't breathe.*
*Momma, Momma.*

Is this the world I want to see?
Is this the world I want to see?

# A GLORIOUS POETIC RAGE

THIS            moment of awakened silence

precious life pulsing through me
        praetorian guards advance

crushing through my solace
        *"damn it, do something"*

                        but there are those who refuse to hear

                history implodes through camera lens
filling each moment with fear

Life is                          NOT

                resistance without change

        days darken in cold iron shackles
        awaken blindfolded privilege

                                *"whose monuments matter"*?

I stretch my life in response            alone

# GROWING UP IN MEMPHIS

I remember the rear
"colored entrance"
at my dentist's office.
I remember seeing
maids walk to the
back of the bus.
I remember hearing
cheers for James Earl Ray.
I remember being denied
promotion 3x as a result
of affirmative action.
I remember telling a racist
joke while visiting Oregon
and no one laughed.
I remember when Martin
became the new
King of Memphis.

I never witnessed white
pointed hoods or crosses
that burned. I never had a
high school classmate of
a different skin color. I
never entered a restaurant
then denied food, drink,
or service. I never read about
Black or Native American History.
I never lived next door to someone
of a different race.

I don't remember my abhorrence
for inequality. I don't remember
standing down a racial joke.
I don't remember being
homeschooled about racism.
I don't remember being stopped by
police while walking home.

I don't remember not being
able to breathe.
I don't remember ever really
giving a shit.

Until I did.

# BUCKET LIST

He said at 98 he was ready to go.

So I asked my hospice patient
if he had done everything on his
bucket list.

"Bucket list?" he asked.

"It's a 'list' of things, places, events
you do before you...you know...*go.*"

He asked for something to write with and
for some fresh instant coffee.

When I returned with his coffee, he was
gently slumped over, pen still in hand,
having written on his paper napkin-


*You are my bucket list. Goodb*

# OPINIONS

I have one but seldom asked for it.
There is no need to borrow mine
since you already have your own.

Some folks have stronger ones,
while others either don't have one or
don't care one way or another.

The stronger yours is, the less likely
you will listen to mine-
or anyone's for that matter.

Brave ones ink theirs deep into
the flesh while the cowards carry them
with torches and rapid-fire weapons.

Free speech says I am entitled to mine,
but it doesn't say I am entitled. That's where
the cowards get confused.

Yogi Berra said it best, "It ain't the heat,
it's the humility."

# AMERICAN HANDICAP

I walk through this café door
to hear an unfamiliar language.

A family or maybe a few close friends
seated in a couched circle
talking about the weather or news back home--

how could I possibly know?

I want to join in, say hello,
to agree or disagree,
share some news of my own
in their natural tongue.

But all I can do is listen,
continue to write this poem, smile and nod
as they rise to leave for wherever
and then--

# A CRACK IN THE CEILING

You showed up this morning without
an invitation or notice
of your intentions.

And why the library ceiling
near the street-side corner window?
A pristine space before you spread
your suffering scar.

Like the one I carry around
in a side pocket so I can forget
who left it without an invitation or
that it even exists.

Please promise not to hurt me
so we can sit together and talk.
I'll share how I became broken
and you can do the same.

And when we are finished,
I'll go about my brokenness
and you can go about yours.
You can stay as long as you want.
You just can't stay here.

# ALMOST FAMOUS: A TRUE STORY

At age 5, I created a character,
taller and thinner than I would ever be.
And famous.

Famous like having to wear a hat and shades
in public, like when everyone
knows your name.

At 10, I was the first to be chosen
in pick-up basketball. At 12, I had my choice
of girls to walk home after school.

But the older I got, the less famous I became.
My girlfriend even dumped me for Billy Hardcastle
who had hair like hers only longer.

It was on a Saturday, helping a stranded motorist
move her stalled car through a busy intersection,
when he pulled up and stopped next to me.

Sunglasses hid his eyes. He asked me if he could help
and for a moment I was hoping he would recognize me,
call me by my name, ask me for an autograph.

But the intersection cleared, so did the stranded motorist,
as my ego stood naked in public watching
Elvis Presley drive off into the evening.

# THE WINDOW

The poet sits at the kitchen table
sipping hot coffee, and writes what is seen outside—
trees, traffic, mountains, molehills.

The poet's window can be a Freida Kahlo painting,
the cliff's edge at Crater Lake, or
canyons of the human heart.

Yesterday, a stranger spotted
my tattooed sleeves. They reminded her
of her late husband, whose love for art
bled from the Gallery canvases
to his arms as well.

"Did he have a favorite tattoo," I asked.

Her voice quivered as she placed her left hand
above her heart outlining the shape
of a something small he had tattooed there.
"Stanley called me 'pumpkin'
for the 43 years we were together."

She slowly shifted her gaze to my left hand
pointing to the inked honey bees,
smiled as to affirm their healing energy,
then turned and walked away
while the window gently closed.

# ROCKETMAN

The circular rim towers ten feet high,
    summons the young lad to hit its mark.
  And, at only 3 feet tall, the boy stands
*frozen*
    from the distance he must conquer.
  Red and Black surround the playground
    as he retrieves his weapon
and embraces it against a tiny chest.
He eyes wood-colored lines
    *hesitates*
then stands at the greater distance.
    One dribble...two dribbles...knees bent
far enough apart so he could
        *launch*
with small hands and a tentative grip.
    He stares as his missile arches upward,
rotates twice then
*strikes*
    the nylon with perfect precision.
I have doubted to ever witness
    pure joy,
but I saw it the moment his ball
    *fell*
through the netting onto the hardwood
as he turned
    to *see*
      if I was watching.

# HERKIE'S SHOE SHOP

Bright as a ripe tomato, this hat
one day floated down from the sky,
landing a bit off-center on my head.
It was a gift from my Uncle Herkie,
short for Herbert,

who owned Herkie's Shoe Repair
in Holly Springs, Mississippi,
next door to Tidwell's Pharmacy
and Soda Shop, where you could wait
for your shoe polish to dry.

When Herkie was younger--
my age younger,
he fell from his barnyard roof
breaking his neck, completely
sauntering it to his head.

For Herkie to look directly at you,
he would have to turn his whole
body either left or right.
To save energy, he just
stared at what was in front of him.

The first thing you noticed
when walking into Herkie's Shop
was the leather smell, old shoes
all lined up on the shelves
waiting on soles or heels or a shine.

A half-smoked cigarette dangled
from the corner of his mouth and the hat
tilted slightly right
on his slightly crooked head.

Herkie was an expert on soles,
replacing them when they were worn
or comforting them when worn out,
the old ones who tended to walk
on the sides of their feet.

He often fell asleep holding his crutches,
mostly on his farmhouse front porch,
where he lived with my Grandmother,
some chickens, cows, and a Rooster
he called Henry.

One Sunday after a roast beef lunch,
I found him sitting there alone, nodding off,
a trail of ashes dangling from his half-smoked
Pall Mall. I interrupted his snooze to ask,
"Uncle Herkie, does your neck hurt much?"

And before I could move in front of him,
he turned his entire body to the left,
his head and neck like petrified wood,
and mumbled as not to disturb his smoke,
"It only hurts, boy, when I think about it".

And that's why I love wearing a hat,
this red one, that floated down in 1965
from a barnyard roof, went up to the heavens
and floated back down again.

# THE SISTER I NEVER HAD

It is her concentration that immediately draws me in,
right index finger follow words on a page, left foot
crossed gently over her right, and wearing
single strap slippers straight out of Oz.

I approach her, curious to know what she is reading,
and wonder if she might give me permission to sit
with her and to share my childhood story of

the sister I never had. How she resemble hers. How she
might teach me what a boy needs to know about girls,
feelings, sugar and spice and all that's nice.

How she loves to play tag football only to tackle me
when I have the carry. How she tells me if my clothes
don't match before we leave for school or if my worn
shoelaces are untied or if I forgot to wear a belt.

I would have called her Matilda. She would be older,
not by much, so we would always be close. She would be
the total tomboy, able to out throw, out climb, or outrace
me by a city mile.

Instead, I'm blessed with girl cousins from different cities.
One who played tackle football in our gridiron front yard,
two who always came to visit at Thanksgiving and others
who taught me how to milk a farm cow at 5 a.m.

As my story came to an end, Matilda never once looked up
and out of the book she was reading, guessing it was about
Charlotte's Web, Alice's Wonderland, or how to become
President.

I slowly stood to say goodbye knowing she would be here
tomorrow, same time and place, this stilled sculpture of
innocence and beauty, of the sister I never had.

# KARI'S STORY

I met *Ed in childhood. His ribs stuck out
like my brother's did.
Grade school and High School,
College then Grad, Ed was always there.
At night and on the weekends too.
He would tell me things,
things like, "It's not safe to play outside".
I believed him, mostly.

Once on Halloween,
Ed dressed up like the devil,
only it wasn't dress up. It was for real.
In my mind.
In my thoughts of joining him
in the bad neighborhood where he lived.
Whenever I would runaway to hide,
I could still hear his laughter
like a clown
who just played a horrible trick.

One night, I heard a voice say,
*"You have everything you need".*
Only it wasn't Ed. It was my breath
under the covers, silencing my mind
so that I could awaken. Not from sleep,
but from failing to be aware
that thinking and being aware of thinking
are two different things.

When I tried explaining this to Ed,
he laughed louder, crushing my ears.
He laughed so loud,
green snot shot out of one nostril
then he snorted the phlegm
back up and into his lungs.
I watched him choking.
I wanted him to die.

As Ed bent over gasping for breath,
I slammed my right palm down onto his back
and watched as he vomited
all of my fears, all of my stories,

all he had convinced me were true
but were not.
I smelled death on his breath.

I wiped his mouth
with freshly painted nails
before clawing 3 words
deep into his cold, dead chest:

*"I am safe".*

*Ed is a fictional character from bipolar illness

# BROTHERLY LOVE

In December of '58, I wrote a letter to Santa asking him
to bring me a little sister for my 6<sup>th</sup> Christmas.

Instead, he brought a Johnny Reb Cannon, two pairs of
socks, and a new freckled-faced little brother.

I already had a little brother so confused as to why Santa
figured I needed another one?

We had the same color eyes, different body types, and
we parted our hair on opposite sides.

Growing up as siblings, we weren't exactly close. Six years
is quite the gap, like the old one between my front teeth.

When he was around ten, Doug had memorized the entire
encyclopedia, as well as the chords to Rocky Mountain High.

His recollection was especially handy whenever I had an overdue
book report or if I needed a song to impress a first date.

His room was down the hall, so breaking and entering mine then
wiping his fingerprints from my LPs was his secret until now.

He once told me that I was "in love with being in love".
Turns out, he was right.

And watching him write complicated computer code, I always
figured he was too intelligent to ever be that social.

Turns out I was wrong. He found heartfulness in the days following
the loss of our father, as I did after the loss of my wife.

I will never forget the three most comforting words he
has ever spoken to me after I called that October morning,

*"We're coming brother".*

We now live many miles apart, but distance will never replace the bond that only brothers know...

We look out for each other, brotherly love.

# THE BANG-BANG MAN

He was a tower of a man
to ten-year old Lone Ranger wannabees,
each Summer trimming the neighbor's hedges and vines.

Dressed in overalls highlighting his muscular arms,
wearing a green John Deere hat, we were out-gunned
by his wood-handled weapon.

Standing between us and the taste of sweet honeysuckles,
we would draw our water pistols when he lowered his over-
sized scissors down and away from the vines.

With one glance in our direction, we would fire a stream of water
as we yelled, "*Bang-Bang*", then watch him grab his chest and
return fire with both thumbs up and forefingers out.

"*Bang-Bang yourself,*" he would shout, letting out a laugh before
returning to his labor. One Summer, he failed to show and all of
the seasons to follow. We never saw him again.

It saddens me to think some other gunslinger wannabee, badged and
armed with something to prove, ignored his innocent surrender,
hands up, and ended our game forever.

To three young cowboys in search of true heroes, one settled for a
star quarterback and the other, an All Star fast-baller. And for a
couple of humid, honeysuckle summers, the Bang-Bang Man was
mine.

# THE DEATH OF THE HANDWRITTEN LETTER

Every Sunday evening, my mother would sit at the
kitchen table and write a 2-page letter, in long-hand,
to her mother who I called Nanny.

I asked her once what she was writing and she said
"adult stuff", so I never asked again.

When I was 16, Nanny died and mother's weekly letters
stopped. And that was the beginning of the end of
the handwritten letter.

Then, there were no computers, internet, text messages
or send buttons to speak about your day, your marriage, or
in my mother's case, her struggle with nicotine.

Today, we type, text, delete, cut, paste, or save a draft if
we happen not to finish. Lovers leave lovers electronically
and "reply all" is a nightmare to corporate ladder-climbers.

I preferred a handwritten note from former bosses but often
had to toot my own horn before they could use it as a spittoon.

Maybe most meaningful note was one I discovered months after
my spouse passed away.  Hidden in back of the pantry sat a
half-filled container with a sticky note in her handwriting:

*Barley*

   *1 Cup Barley*
   *3 Cups Water*

# SOME QUESTIONS I HAVE ABOUT LEAP YEAR

Where does February actually go when it leaps and
why does it leap only every four years? These are
some questions I have about Leap Year.

A frog leaps one space at a time, even when
jumping out of boiling water. The same with
the Chess Pawn, but the King

must castle for permission to leap more. Jack needed
one leap to conquer the candlestick and we watched
Neil take a giant one to save all mankind.

But what if February leaped every two years instead?
Some folks would be twice as old I guess,
probably dead by now.

If Julius Caesar had been born on the 29th,
after 3 Centuries without leaping, we would
celebrate New Year's Day in July.

That's because the Earth's rotation is not fast enough
to completely circle the Sun in 365 days. Instead,
we're stuck with this extra day every four years.

Personally, I would be more satisfied with an
extra helping of mashed potatoes and gravy
when we celebrate Thanksgiving in May.

# HUNTERS AND FARMERS

Hunters hunt
Farmers farm

Hunters seek
Farmers sow

Hunters attach
Farmers let go

Hunters need
Farmers nourish

Hunters expect
Farmers extend

Hunters pine
Farmers plow

Hunters hurt
Farmers heal

Hunters always hunt
Farmers always farm

And that's all I'll say about relationships & romance.

# TRILLIUM

Rising alone
surrounded by ferns
and forest

Offering a radiance
white trilogy with yellow
and gold

Never alone
unlike the human heart

Reluctant to learn
it only gets the love
that it allows.

# THE WINE WE POUR

The wine we pour
often leaves its chosen container
empty and broken.

Water never turned to wine.
It was the other way around.

Resentment empties us
leaving nothing to patch holes
unkind words have made.

Taste your wine first,
before you serve it to others.

Patch your fluke with
stitches of forgiveness.

Love, even when
there is little left to pour.

# TO SIT AT THE COFFEE BAR

Black coffee and water
the grinder grinding
the steamers steaming
maroon-ringed saucer
catching thoughts thrown
out of a cavernous cup
He can't help but stare
at the emptiness after
each sip He can't help
but wonder if he needs
a refill then becomes
confused about love
the willingness to show it
accept it get lost in it
savor it like this dark
liquid steamed scent like
the smell of her skin

# THEN THERE ARE WOLVES

They prey.
Preying is what they do.
Carnivores of fool's flesh.

Nocturnal animals.
Stealers of time.
Reapers becoming

> *bottom-feeders*
> *of your shame*
> *you won't see coming.*

Too late.
One look

> to slit your niceties
> to slice your invites
> to leave you bleeding

with their lack of
genuine interest
this time, next time
every goddamn time.

Walk away, keep walking.
Be the Farmer never the Hunter
Fool me once is once enough.

> there is no try in friendship
> *there are friends*
> *then there are wolves.*

# NOT WHAT YOU WANTED BUT WHAT YOU GOT

When        things get        quiet.

      When      mothers try   to rescue   you

but can't     Shoved down     crawling out

     The smell of leather   The buckle   welts your skin

That's when   you wish   you had not been   born

     That's when   you wish   you had a   gun

Not   what you wanted   but what you   got.

# DIATRIBE

There is a            space
where the heart takes refuge
from the piercings of others
who give away their suffering
being blind to it
without cane or seeing eye dog
trampling over tenderness
until love captures a respite breath
to simply survive.

We need that         space,
we pine for it like a Beggar
on bleeding knees hungers for food,
like lost love grieves what might have been,
like a thief pleads for mercy in the crimson
court where the Judger is sentenced
and the Beggar goes free.

# WHILE TRAVELING EAST TO WEST

Whose grave markers pave
these highways--
crosses, flowers, dates?

How did each journey end?
Each being, someone's
child, parent, lover, friend.

Did they perish alone, become lost
in the night and never witness
another rising sun?

And now a young fawn
lying sideways, half-in, half-out
of the road--

where will her grave marker be?

# STYROFOAM

White, stiff structures
Inserts hold other structures
Packed like sardines suffocating
Taped together - no escape
Millions, millions of cancer cells
Explode on my body as I rip them open
Little dots of leukemia resist my touch
Not to disturb their interruptions into
My obsessive, compulsiveness

about the small stuff

Overnight dishes left in the sink,
Refrigerator management of
Spoiled leftovers, meats, and milk
Each are teachers, mentors, reminders
That life is about

loving the small stuff

White particles floating
Dirty dishes dancing
Avocados ripening
It's 7 p.m. and the sun is still ripening.

# COUNTING

A Homeless man sits
on the end of a park bench
covered by a heavy woolen coat
and dearth
digs deep into his pant pocket
with fingerless gloves
to count his silver treasure
then stops...suddenly sensing
that counting coins
is easier
than loving himself.

# THE GEESE AT LACAMAS

lake
are not
necessarily beautiful,
strutting about with their long
necks, white sidewall faces, and bloated
bodies until they lift in flight, forming that
imperfect "V", one side longer than the other,
speaking a language that transforms them, unlike
Lila, daughter of a shoemaker or her husband, Stefano,
son of a grocer, who Lila despises, who can't seem to keep
his hands in his own pants, but more like Nino, son of a poet,
who Lila loves in spite of his temper who becomes the father of
her child, the father he never knew, the father he thought he
could  never be, but becomes.
Beautiful like that.

# TRASH DAY

It's Trash Day
and I hear glass breaking.

Luckily, I remembered
to sit out all the empties--

Tall ones, short ones, thick ones,
even some with very last drops.

Like moments in our lives-

opened
   used
      shelved
         emptied
            trashed

some shattered, but not broken.

# USED BOOKS

They usually occupy the entry space or front wall
as you enter the bookstore or in this coffee shop
where I sit inside Powell's City of Books--

a Portlandian paradise of bound paper and prices,
in alphabetical order, luring consummate readers
to their favorite writers- Grafton, Clancy, Munro,
Rowling, or Elmore Leonard to name a few.

They wait motionless for a new owner like a
kenneled pup waits having once been adopted
then abandoned by someone else in some other place.

Hardbacks, paperbacks, all highlighted treasures
like this edition of *Hombre*, an old favorite
with an inside cover inscription that reads,
"*To John Russell: Long Live Mescal- Elmore*".

Most days, I could pass for one of the used editions-
touched, bought, read, shelved, sold or tossed,
maybe re-purposed as a doorstop or a make-shift lift
for a laptop to take the screen to perfect camera level.

Today, I want to be the first book off of the shelve,
held again by desiring hands, thumbed through by
delicate fingers, adopted by new parents, then taken home
to a cozy bedroom with a French door balcony.

In the evening, I want to rest atop an oak nightstand,
wait to be opened, held, and caressed before being gently
placed across my owner's breasts as she falls asleep and dreams.

# THE PERFECT COUNTRY & WESTERN POEM

If the perfect Country & Western song
is about trains, trucks, getting drunk, and prison,
what might Mama say makes the perfect
Country & Western poem?

Would it rhyme with every line or
skip a line or two? Would vowels
and consonants alliterate or assonate?

Would it have a mix of metaphors and
similes like a mile-high ice cream cone or
would it be full of hyperboles?

Would it be a sonnet, a limerick, a quatrain
or haiku, or maybe iambic pentameters written
in isometric lines?

According to Mama,

*"the perfect Country & Western poem would
call me by my name, let me hang around as long
as I want to, even stand naked out in the rain."*

And just reading this,
it's all I can do to keep from crying.

# A PURE LITTLE INNOCENT BEING
*for Marta*

There can be no order of birth
and the angels never rest
when grace becomes the work.

A pure little innocent being,
a precious second son
we were unable to fix.

We took his pain and made it ours,
to be by his side and into his years
with a divine labor of love.

We held his breath in our hands
when his lungs and body
took to their rest,

We drank, wept, and bathed in
tears of tenderness when cradling
him and impossible odds.

Luke's love captures every heart who
meets him. Words are never enough
to describe his sweet presence.

There can be no order of birth
and the angels never rest
when grace becomes the guru.

# I WALKED AMOUNG THE DEAD TODAY

in a cemetery of stirring souls anxious for attention.

Carlson was celebrating his 90th and Franks, a fresh

bouquet of flowers. Ferguson had fought the good fight

and Mr. & Mrs. Riales were resting in peace together.

As I entered, I respectfully removed my hat. It was easier

than taking a knee, the right one that died 3 years earlier.

The air became hauntingly still and a slight breeze began

blowing flags, the small ones decorating simple graves.

I sat on a bench next to the urn lockers and wondered why

the ashes were stored and not spread.

Suddenly, the cottonwoods started floating their buds in

the direction of the exit and the thought arose that maybe

it was time for me to go... home, that is.

# THE RAIN IN WASHINGTON STATE

Everybody here complains about the rain.
Well, maybe not everybody, just those who
didn't grow up in the Pacific Northwest.

The first thing I learned when moving
to Washington State is never complain
about the rain.

The one (and only) time I did,
I was schooled by a born-and-raised
who said "That's what ball caps are for!"

The second thing I learned is how to spot a visitor.
It's actually quite easy since they will be
the only ones carrying an umbrella.

Folks in Washington State never complain about
the rain. They only complain about those who
complain about the rain.

They also never complain about the heat or
humidity, primarily because there is none.
Air conditioning is considered as
an unnecessary expense.

There's something soothing about the
cool, crisp, wet morning air that makes
heat and humidity unnecessary.

Besides, hats and hoodies
are a hell of a lot cheaper than
a brand new two-ton Goodman.

# CAMAS

*cam.as \ pronounced kam-us*

Named after the lily flower Native Americans used to make their bread and molasses, Camas was the first American town north of the Columbia River.

A papermill city in SW Washington, Camas shares the Columbia with Portland, OR, and a border with Washougal, WA.

*wa.shou.gal \ pronounced wa-shoe-gull.*

Henry Pittock built the papermill in 1883, establishing the Columbia River Paper Company, only to re-build it two-years later after it was destroyed by fire.

Today, we have Henry to thank each time we set our dinner tables using paper napkins.

Camas is the Pacific Northwest version of Gatlinburg, TN and possesses the combined magic of Eureka Springs and Mountain Home, AR.

Growing up in the South, I never believed in magic until I drove through the Historic Downtown District and immediately knew Camas was home.

I was told the paper mill releases an unpleasant odor described as something between "rotten eggs and sour milk" and that we are due a volcano from Saint Helens any day now.

Turns out, the only odors I've experienced are cooked bacon from Natalia's Cafe, fresh coffee from Hidden River Roasters and Caffe Piccolo and IPA hops from Caps-n-Taps.

Within a stone's throw is Squeeze & Grind if I fancy a smoothie, Nuestra Mesa for some Mex spiciness, an array of flavors from Navidis Oils, or garden gifts from the Wednesday Farmer's Market.

You might even spot a mindful poet, who left the Cumberland for the Columbia, the humidity for the rain, mosquitoes for cottonwoods, and the Titans for the Pride of the Papermakers.

# THE BELLS AT NOON

Four quarter notes ring from a distance
Two high and two low
Again, then
A dozen more to follow

Yesterday
I counted them forward
From one to twelve
Ended in a hallowed
*Haunting*

Today
I count them backward
From twelve to one
To one from twelve
Never saying zero

Four quarter notes ring from a distance
Two high and two low
I count them backward
Never saying zero
Never growing old

# CONSTANT SORROW

They mostly start around 5:30 a.m. after next door
neighbors leave for work and end in the early
evening when they return.

They come and go but never more than
a three-beat rest in-between.

Some days to amuse myself, I try and place them
as words in a familiar song. Yesterday, it was
Jingle Bells or was it Hell's Bells?

If I leave out to take a walk, they immediately
get louder.

Recently, one neighbor asked if I could hear him
running up and down his staircase. In the Pacific
Northwest, that's one alternative to running or
walking outside during the rainy season.

"No, the only thing I ever hear is your dog barking!"

One might think that would be the end of it as I
watch him leave for work then
begin singing, "Oh Brother, Where Art Thou."

# COLD BREW

Baristas say
it is the strongest pour

iced with a hint of
sweet almond milk

10 ounces
stirred not shaken

unlike Nell who needs
to      *chill*

from her winless war with
rage

racing to cross
an imaginary finish line

then awarded
a bronze medal migraine

slowly sipped

# WHEN YOU DON'T WRITE

When you don't write
it's like clinging to thin air
with an open hand.
Birds seems to know all the words
each morning when they sing them
onto empty pages.
The man passed out
in the grassy spot
outside my second story window
hears them and moans.
He desperately
tries to stand
but his knees refuse
to follow his hips.
When you don't write
you fall face first
on the front foyer floor,
rise slowly,
gently stroke your side
like the tender skin
of a mother's breast.
Now, all I can do is sit here
and watch as the blank page
begins to beckon me again.

# HOW YOU DO ANYTHING
## IS HOW YOU DO EVERYTHING

I *vacuum* the floor to build my triceps
I *rake* the leaves to rake the leaves
I *drive* over the speed limit to avoid boredom
I *eat* with the opposite hand to know the feeling of being handicapped
I *hold* my head out the car window to think out loud
I *take* a shower and a bath at the same time
I *poach* an egg because I can
I *don't sleep late* because I can't
I *crunch* cough drops to contemplate
I *speak* to a stranger when I feel alone
I *read* so that I am never alone
I *order* espresso to pronounce it correctly (*repeat* with salmon)
I *write* so I can stay on the safe side of sanity
I *curse* to keep from becoming angry
I *laugh* to kill all of my demons
I *cry* to hold someone else's pain
I *get tattooed* to feel more pain than what I am holding
I *walk* to appreciate those that cannot
I *drink coffee* to know addiction
I *get up early* to hear passing trains
I *worry* about not much of anything at my age
I *want to bake* everything at 375 degrees
I *wear* the same thing 2 days in a row
I *think* dust bunnies are angel poop
I *don't have* a dog so I teach myself to stay
I *hike* to help keep the forest alive
I *scream* at racists and bigots
I *meditate* to notice my mind making stuff up
I *sleep* with the cover sheet upside down
I *wear* a mask to protect myself and others from a deadly virus
I *end* my poems with-

# ABOUT ATMOSPHERE PRESS

Atmosphere Press is an independent, full-service publisher for excellent books in all genres and for all audiences. Learn more about what we do at atmospherepress.com.

We encourage you to check out some of Atmosphere's latest releases, which are available at Amazon.com and via order from your local bookstore:

*Big Man Small Europe*, poetry by Tristan Niskanen
*In the Cloakroom of Proper Musings,* a lyric narrative by Kristina Moriconi
*Lucid_Malware.zip*, poetry by Dylan Sonderman
*The Unordering of Days,* poetry by Jessica Palmer
*It's Not About You,* poetry by Daniel Casey
*A Dream of Wide Water,* poetry by Sharon Whitehill
*Radical Dances of the Ferocious Kind*, poetry by Tina Tru
*The Woods Hold Us,* poetry by Makani Speier-Brito
*My Cemetery Friends: A Garden of Encounters at Mount Saint Mary in Queens, New York*, nonfiction and poetry by Vincent J. Tomeo
*Report from the Sea of Moisture,* poetry by Stuart Jay Silverman
*The Enemy of Everything*, poetry by Michael Jones
*The Stargazers,* poetry by James McKee
*The Pretend Life*, poetry by Michelle Brooks
*Minnesota and Other Poems*, poetry by Daniel N. Nelson
*Interviews from the Last Days*, sci-fi poetry by Christina Loraine

# ABOUT THE AUTHOR

Elmo Shade currently facilitates mindfulness-based education and curriculum development for e-Mindful based in Orlando, FL. He earned a Certified Mindfulness Teacher Professional (CMT-P) designation from the International Mindfulness Teachers Association (IMTA).

Elmo received his formal mindfulness training from the Center for Mindfulness at UMass Medical Center, Vanderbilt Osher Center for Integrative Medicine, Duke Center for Integrative Medicine, Google's Search Inside Yourself Leadership Development Program, and the Institute of Mindful Leadership.

Elmo is also a poet and an unapologetic coffee addict. He currently volunteers his spare time with Meals on Wheels in Washougal, WA and with the Camas Downtown Association in Camas, WA.

He is the author of *Standing On One Leg: Poems of Love, Loss, & the Spaces In-Between (2017) and Coffee Grinds: Poems & Stories for the Less Than Perfect Soul (2019).*

Feel free to contact him at elmo@elmoshade.com.

# AUTHOR'S NOTE

It is important to note that many of the poems contained in this manuscript were written during the COVID-19 Pandemic and Black Lives Matter Movement and were intended to raise the collective consciousness of a nation in economic and physical health peril. I am grateful for you, as a reader, and to Atmosphere Press for publishing this third poetry collection. All proceeds from the sales of this book will be donated to Meals on Wheels and M4BL.

elmo shade, August 2020

Also available on Amazon Books:

CPSIA information can be obtained
at www.ICGtesting.com
Printed in the USA
LVHW090345100221
678885LV00006B/1028